Thanks for all of
your support. ♡

Words Beget Action

Jennifer M. Gonzalez

Hello, my name is Monae and sometimes when my baby brother is crying and whining... I wish it was just me and mommy again.

I HAVE TWO YOUNGER SIBLINGS. AT FIRST I THOUGHT HAVING A LITTLE SISTER WAS GOING TO BE SO MUCH FUN AND IT IS BUT, SHE CAN BE KIND OF ANNOYING TOO SOMETIMES AND NOW THAT WE HAVE A BABY

BROTHER; MOMMY MUST SPLIT HER TIME BETWEEN ME, SISSY AND LITTLE BROTHER.

I DON'T KNOW HOW SHE DOES IT BECAUSE SHE IS ALWAYS COOKING, DOING HER HOMEWORK OR

CLEANING; SHE'S LIKE A REAL-LIFE SUPERWOMAN. MAYBE BEING AN ONLY CHILD WOULDN'T HAVE BEEN SO BAD AFTER ALL. HMM...

NINE YEARS AGO WHEN MOMMY WAS PREGNANT WITH RENEE, I COULDN'T WAIT FOR HER TO COME OUT SO I COULD TEACH HER THINGS; SHE WAS GOING TO BE MY OWN PERSONAL BABY DOLL.

I WAS GOING TO FEED HER, CHANGE HER PAMPERS, DRESS HER UP AND PROTECT HER LIKE A GOOD BIG SISTER. I STILL DO BUT OUR FIRST INTRODUCTION WAS SO WEIRD. THE FIRST TIME I LAID EYES ON RENEE I

CRIED BECAUSE MOMMY CALLED HER "SNICKERDOODLE" AND ALTHOUGH I DIDN'T QUITE KNOW WHAT IT MEANT, IT MADE ME FEEL LIKE MOMMY WOULD NEVER GIVE ME ANOTHER CUTE NICKNAME LIKE THAT AGAIN. I WAS

SOOO JEALOUS.
   I WANTED HER TO GO BACK TO THE BABY FACTORY. HAVE YOU EVER FELT THIS WAY ABOUT YOUR BABY BROTHER OR SISTER?

Renee and I are six years apart so now that I am 14 years old, we don't have as much in common. I mean, sometimes I will sit and watch television shows with her and then we have

FAMILY GAME NIGHTS WITH MOMMY SO THAT WE ALL CAN BOND BUT BESIDES THAT, I DON'T SPEND MUCH TIME WITH HER.

I HAVE TO DO SOMETHING ABOUT THAT. MOMMY IS

ALWAYS TELLING ME THAT THE BOND BETWEEN SISTERS IS SO SPECIAL AND HOW LUCKY I AM BUT I JUST THINK ABOUT ALL OF THE THINGS I COULD HAVE AND COULD DO IF I DIDN'T HAVE SIBLINGS. KIND OF SELFISH OF ME,

HUH? WELL, LET'S TALK ABOUT THAT LITTLE BROTHER OF MINE.

MAXWELL IS THE CUTEST LITTLE BROTHER. HE HAS THE MOST HANDSOME LITTLE CHUNKY FACE AND HE IS

ALWAYS SMILING; I LOVE THAT ABOUT HIM BUT EVERY SO OFTEN, I WILL FIND HIM IN THE BEDROOM CRYING, YELLING OR FUSSING BECAUSE HE IS HUNGRY, WET OR HE JUST WANTS ATTENTION. WERE WE ALL LIKE THAT?

GEESH, HE EATS AND SLEEPS MORE THAN ANY PERSON I HAVE EVER MET BEFORE AND I SLEEP A WHOLE LOT.

BEFORE RENEE AND MAXWELL WERE BORN, MOMMY

AND I SPENT A LOT MORE ONE ON ONE TIME AND I MISS THAT. WE STILL GO ON FAMILY VACATIONS AND PRETTY MUCH ANYTHING THAT I ASK FOR I USUALLY GET BECAUSE I MAKE REALLY GOOD GRADES IN SCHOOL

BUT I KNOW WE WOULD DO A LOT MORE IF I DIDN'T HAVE RENEE AND MAXWELL TAGGING ALONG EVERY PLACE WE WENT. SOMETIMES MOMMY LOOKS SO TIRED BECAUSE SHE IS ALWAYS BUSY AND HELPS EVERYONE

WHO ASKS WHENEVER SHE CAN; I ADMIRE THAT ABOUT HER. SOMETIMES I ASK HER IF SHE NEEDS ANYTHING OR IF SHE'S ALRIGHT BECAUSE I JUST WANT HER TO SMILE A LITTLE MORE.

SHE USUALLY SAYS SHE IS OKAY, I HOPE SHE REALLY IS OKAY. I JUST WANT TO LET YOU KNOW THAT HAVING SIBLINGS IS A GREAT THING. IT'S NORMAL TO FEEL LIKE YOU NEED TIME TO YOURSELF SOMETIMES OR THAT

YOU JUST WANT TO SPEND A LITTLE TIME WITH YOUR PARENT(S) BY YOURSELF; IT DOESN'T MEAN YOU LOVE YOUR SIBLINGS ANY LESS... IT JUST MEANS, YOU ARE HUMAN AND THERE ARE SO MANY BOYS AND GIRLS IN

THE WORLD THAT FEEL THE SAME WAY AS YOU. CONTINUE TO LOVE YOUR SIBLINGS AND ENJOY GROWING UP TOGETHER BECAUSE WE WON'T ALWAYS BE THIS YOUNG AND MOMMY ALWAYS TELLS ME THAT

ONE DAY I AM GOING TO WISH I COULD GET THE TIME BACK I SHARED WITH THEM.

THE

END

Made in the USA
Columbia, SC
23 May 2019